ORDINARY OMENS

※

LeAnn Bjerken

A Publication of The Poetry Box®

Poems © 2024 LeAnn Bjerken
All rights reserved

Editing & Book Design by Shawn Aveningo Sanders
Cover Design by Robert R. Sanders (RobertSandersCreative.com)

No part of this book may be republished without permission
from the author, except in the case of brief quotations
embodied in critical essays, epigraphs, reviews and articles,
or publisher/author's marketing collateral.

ISBN: 978-1-956285-68-0
Published in the United States of America
Wholesale Distribution by Ingram Group

Published by The Poetry Box,® September 2024
Portland, Oregon, United States
website: ThePoetryBox.com

*For Steve and Eowyn,
you open the doors and hold my hands on this magical journey.*

Contents

The Magician	7
Luck of the Pisces	8
Scrying	10
Paper Airplane	11
Love Awaiting Burial	12
Fortuna Major	13
Making	14
Floromancy	15
Knot Magic	16
Birthday Candles	17
The Rabbit	18
Holds	19
Orinthomancy	20
Talisman	21
The Lovers	22
Keep on Floating	23
Faith	25
Cephalonomancy	26
The Chrysalis	28
Future Female Guppy	29
Blue Eyes	31
Remember Breakfast	32
On Rice	33
Dandelion	34
Dowsing	35
The Great American Eclipse	36
We Were Like the Birds	37
Prophet	38
Acknowledgments	41
Early Praise	43
About the Author	45

The Magician

Bright stars chart the place, glass sands stir the hour
steady your mind, believe in its power.

Summon earth, air, water, and fire
then gaze within to find your desire.

Raise in your hand the wand's golden flame
your body a bridge linking heaven and earth.
Hover in place, forget your name,
mystical seeker of knowledge and worth.

The red rose of passion, the lily pure white
now flourish entwined as if one.
The way shines brightest when lit by the moon
as it chases, then veils the path of the sun.

As is above, so too below
whisper in secret one wish, and one woe.

Spin twice in a ring, then count to three
and as you will it, so now shall it be.

Luck of the Pisces

I was born near the Ides of March

the day before the day
we celebrate the patron saint of Ireland.

I'm told I weighed 9 lbs. or so
my mother's cyan fish eyes peering

out of a head far too large
to match my tiny body.

Golden hair that grew out slowly
in spun sugar wisps

like the delicate wings of a flying fish.

I remember the four-wheeler accident
that almost left me scarred.

Dad said I was lucky
when he ran to hold me in his arms

after I'd lost my helmet, and half the skin of my cheek
to the shingles of a low built barn roof.

But there is no outward blemish,
you tell me I am beautiful

and I know you wonder why
I never see myself that way.

It's probably just the little girl in me,

who remembers boys that never passed love notes
and girls who snickered at my clothes.

Maybe there was something in that piece of cheek
perhaps the thickest skin I ever had

a scaly island that took months to heal,
loosening inside and finally floating away

in the pool one day mid swimming lesson.

Scrying

I am always
just under the surface

and the ghosts that I call arms
stretch ahead of me.

Glancing above
I see them reflected in the darkly mirrored ceiling.

I stroke inward

letting my hands come together in a prayer
before they fly from me like birds on rippled glass

a thin green wave
breaking into cool air.

My eyes level with the sunset
my body still, submerged
my breath barely rising to meet the waves.

Diving is a way of letting go
asking the blue to pull you down

for a moment.

And the space inside is but a shadow,
a mouth searching for its lake-filled voice

with echoed answers floating out
like dead leaves to the surface.

Paper Airplane

Once we were born with feathers
and voices that spoke of wind

lifting away from the world
shredding fear like wisps of cloud underfoot

following an old song.

Then just as suddenly we were naked,
plucked and scrubbed clean.

We ached with longing for the open-skied spaces
and a sweet hunger slept within us.

But clumsy hands have folded that thin, pulp dream
into a shining, solid, vessel

and these alloy wings will carry us
higher than ever before.

But is this the place
we've envisioned,

and where will we land
when we fall once more?

Love Awaiting Burial

When she wants love she starts by filling up glass jars
and burying them in the backyard at night
like a desperate dog
moving bare bones to safer places.

She's always on the hunt
keeping her pantry well stocked with all manner of grave goods.

She has a hankering for trust and faithfulness
but her passion is a deep red wine with notes of chocolate.

She spends every sunset in the kitchen whipping delight into
   foamy peaks
throwing salt over her shoulder with a whispered kiss.

She'll fill each jar with pickled promises
boiling off the excess desire
leaving them to marinate in sweetness until they're set
the smartly dressed, the freshly canned, awaiting burial.

Then she walks out to the field to dance and dig and chant
while the moon spills down the clouds to blanket the open holes.

She covers each jar with crumbs from her hands
and rakes the topsoil closed with her nails.

She'll lie beside them awhile
holding her breath and pretending she's in the ground too
feeling the spell weave itself to life
drawing from the dark, stirring the roots beneath.

Fortuna Major

There is a science to the way the sand falls
from lightly grasping fingers.

It's the journey rising from underneath,
the loam imprinting patterns on the brain.

Every morning the sun's song kisses the green
and somewhere an egg is hatching.

Below, the earthworms must stay moist to breathe
strong bodies writhing forward, tunneling.

The rabbit's instinct also is to dig and hide
hollowing its secret niche.

Power dances with desire in the dirt that we are made of
shifting in our veins, circling outward.

We're stones cast down the mountain,
seeds borne up and away

rings around a planet
it's golden center smoldering.

Making

We make love out of nothing,

knowing each other's bodies
remembering
the way a child remembers
how to tie his shoes.

We make love with the windows open

our laughter riding the wind
through the neighbor's laundry
wrapping and unwrapping
undulating on the line.

We make love in the heat

each tasting the others skin
fresh as mown grass
or the anticipation of rain.

We make love in the cold

the two of us
eager little birds slamming into window glass
pale white
melting to form one long shape.

We make love out of nothing

a thought that grows in the mind
visions conjured from gesture
words spoken aloud in the night.

Floromancy

Flowers leave a part of their fragrance
on the hands that bestow them.
  —Chinese Proverb

It's all green here now
and we fall open in the sun

relishing the newness of the world
photosynthesizing every detail.

Living color we can see,
silk that we can touch.

Inhale the magic dust
and call it beautiful.

Do you wonder what a flower
asks of its gods?

How much can it still feel
trapped in glass and withering,

drinking water from a tall jar
and slowly becoming the shadow of a stem.

Colors fading, body drying,
the scent of musk and rot.

See it, touch it, hold it,
and call it beautiful.

Knot Magic

I saw it first
how well we go together.

Two kids who both had trouble
learning how to tie their shoes.

We were used to finding
the Velcro solution to every problem

having given up on bunny ear analogies
and easy rhyming long ago.

But some kind of magic united us
because something inside just fits.

Almost as though a young girl wishing for love
once bound her desire up in a cord

and buried it out of sight,
forgotten.

At first it might appear simple,
my end is tied to yours.

But I know we both sometimes feel
when the knots inside pull

painfully but sweetly
and we twist toward each other

on fire with their strength.

Birthday Candles

She can't remember what it was she wanted
and there's only one chance, once a year.

It probably seems silly

but ever since she realized she's pretty,
she wanted to stay young and beautiful.

Find the fountain,
drink the cure.

Well, a girl can dream, but a woman
starts to see too many candles and not enough air.

She notices the wax
falling onto those sweet, frosted peaks

sliding down slowly,
a masterpiece that's melting.

The song begins to end
and everyone is staring expectantly.

She inhales,
the heat building in her face,

one chance
no chance.

Make a wish, they say.
Make a wish!

The Rabbit

When I saw the baby cotton tail
running fast along the sidewalk
streetlights reflected in his eyes

I remembered that night we made
frantic love
on the roof of your van
warm metal pressed against my thighs
unprotected in the summer heat.

With me on my back
did you see the falling stars
reflected in my eyes,
feel the wild heartbeat in my chest
building to a shining scream?

We talked until sunrise
anxious, wondering if we created
a mistake
making promises and
choosing names.

I'd forgotten all of it
until I saw him
passing through dappled light
no grass, just warm pavement under paws
his frantic movement
his wide and fearful eyes

and oh, how I ached to love
so small a thing.

Holds

You hold the fancy napkin
I want to leave my lip prints on
in the pink red that is
Fuchsia dream.

The walls are so pale
I want to mark them too,
pull out my sharpie
to defile them with naughty words
and dirty pictures.

I want to have a food fight
and later eat the leavings off your face
sitting on the floor and giggling until
we can agree on what it is that holds us in
restrains our wildness

makes us seem like
fish dancing on a line
as time around floats on unchanged.

ORINTHOMANCY

Here in the forest
bones have fallen together

sinking like stones through water
too heavy now for flight.

White remnants mixing with pine scent
laid out still, and sharp against mossy earth.

Their pattern a hollowed echo,
a gypsy flutist's breath from deep within

singing of love and lost things.

Trace now the skull's sockets
following the calcified lines.

Let fingers read
the road map left open to the rain.

Above a fern rustles,
it's green feathers mimicking forgotten flesh.

An inauspicious message, gray skies yet to come.

Talisman

She's not the first person to compliment me on my wedding ring,
noticed its fallen star sparkle right away.

She asks how long we've been married,
then how old I was when I first had sex.

I hesitate and she notices that too,
and smiles to herself because she knows
it wasn't you.

I slouch in the chair remembering
how I'd waited until I was nineteen,

how he didn't believe I was a virgin,
like I wouldn't have given him that gift and more for free.

I know he realized
I wanted him to love me.

I felt it the next morning when he asked for his t-shirt back
in a voice that said he wasn't happy to see me wearing it.

But here I am years later,
and it's *your* ring that circles my left finger.

A white gold promise.
A circle so strong it transforms the skin beneath.

It's safe and it's warm,
and I never want to take it off.

The damn nurse can smile all she wants.

The Lovers

The first man and the first woman
stood newly made

in a beautiful garden
with trees of fruit and fire.

Yet their open hands reached
first for one another.

Love, a mountain springing up between them
two tectonic plates shifting together

thrust so tightly upward
it felt like they were one bird flying,

and the woman found herself
trembling and weak.

She sensed the weight of angel eyes gazing down,
but couldn't help hearing the serpent's laughing hiss through
   the leaves

and felt the knotted pull forward
into destiny.

At the end, when they found themselves
expelled from paradise,

she fell in the dirt and cried
remembering how it had tasted.

And he knelt behind her, his hand on her hand
where it held the curve of her belly

one over one, over one.

Keep On Floating

I stay home to climb the walls with you.

We walk the ceiling
tripping in the door frames
stepping around lights.

The shadows of our fingers make faces
as we eat our dinner sideways
squatting on the wall.

We set the stereo and practice dancing,
when you lift me in your arms
I hang below.

Strangers ring the bell,
but we don't answer.

The loose change rains
from our pockets to the floor.

We laugh,
slough off our clothes,
and keep on floating.

We don't concern ourselves with falling.

We're waiting for the world to right itself,
hovering just out of reach.

Here everything stands straight up,
from the tired string of a balloon
to my long brown hair.

[. . .]

The lighter our thoughts,
the more things join us in the air.

Until the whole house is floating
and we're mixed in with all the rest
drifting by.

Faith

A wisp of white magic
that glows like gold

slipping through the fingers
of healing hands

witch's medicine
waving over me.

For an hour I lie listening
as she sings prayers

to the heart of a warrior
lost and wandering in rain.

She ties the feather to a string
looping it around my neck.

It presses softly against my chest
whispering and small.

Later as I sleep in my well-formed nest
of mud and broken shells

I feel the angry fragments
fall away.

Cephalonomancy

A mutual friend told me
the doctors had to cut open your head again.

It's been years since I saw you
but I can easily picture them shaving away
all your brown curls
drilling into your skull
and extracting the probably benign octopus
suction cupped to your brain.

Thinking back, I remember lots of times
when it should have been obvious, but I still don't know
what was wrong with us
what was wrong with you.

You'd think a three-hearted cephalopod in your head
would have taught you something about love.

I always felt everything, and you got high so you wouldn't.

People who knew us then will remind me
that we were only together for a month,
roughly four weeks, I guess.

They say if you're still feeling pain
weeks after an extraction,
you should probably speak to a healer.

It's kind of nice to think that now
they're telling you that instead of me.

When I catch myself missing you I tell myself I'm being idiotic
this ache is nothing serious
that ink blot on the card doesn't resemble your face.

And I wonder what lies you told yourself,
what you felt when they showed you
the octopus
burrowing its length ever deeper into the gray.

I like to think it was there the whole time.

The Chrysalis

I shed my skin a last time
my child soul
sleeping beneath its round room.

Sapphire edges of my forming wings held
in a new cycle of dreaming
waiting to appear.

The murmur of liquefied cells
imagines a new form

paper arms
breaking from their casings.

Finding the world from upside down
new blood rushing into my veins,
I'm preparing to fly.

Watch me breathe
the wet green fear of outside
my delicately dusted skin crawling.

Know that I have only
this little life,
poised on the edge of a fingertip.

Future Female Guppy

She lies drifting

bath tiles becoming a tropical sea
that slides in and out of focus along the tub's porcelain shoulders.

She's thinking of what the tarot reader said

three cards spread out before her
past, present, future

shallow beach behind
instinctively moving into deeper waters

a dark unknown, where living things drift quietly
even now its waiting somewhere beyond the frosted curtain.

Be ready to swim.

Her blood is warm now from the water
baby face scrubbed pink and clean

the foam settles on her like rainbow guppy scales
gently pressing, a heat glowing inside.

So, she lets herself feel it

imagining her skin stretched thin
struggling to hide the millions of orb like eyes beneath.

And they whisper
stories of the bubbles bursting, water draining away

a heart on fire with new love

[. . .]

finding strength in every new struggle
of their tiny minnow tails

mouths open in hunger
in wonder

born ready to swim.

Blue Eyes

Your eyes are blue
like the berries neither of us want in muffins.

Even when we've argued
you circle back

a distant planet
whose contrite cobalt atmosphere calls out to me

the soft weight of icy fingers
molding my fevered skin.

It's disastrously delicious,
and interestingly addictive.

This is old school,
love potion magic,

an arrow in the moonlight
piercing the heart.

I know I shouldn't forgive you just because
you have amazing blue eyes.

I just can't think of a better reason.

Remember Breakfast

I remember when you and I
would spend the day in bed.

Morning would stretch itself into yesterday's clothes
and we'd go out for breakfast in the afternoon.

You gave me the yellow center of your eggs
as we silently agreed to split the hash browns.

I never felt alone
until I felt the sun rise without you.

Now when I wake
the golden finches drop one by one into air.

Their song at the window hesitating
snagged in the curtains.

I watch the world turn fresh coffee new
my hands a waiting cup

an empty breakfast plate.

On Rice

You have rice in your beard
and I have hair in my rice.

It could be cat fur
but I blame you because you cooked.

It must be the hint of Irish
that gives you such fire red stubble
despite your Nordic roots.

I don't know why I love your hair

come to think of it
I've probably eaten whole spoonful's by now.

Nearly ten years into this dish,
I wonder if it's possible to swallow enough of you
to be haunted with your essence
build myself into a voodoo doll from the inside out

share your joys
and feel your pain
as small red beans
on white.

Dandelion

I take my coffee black in the morning
when the dandelions have gone to seed,

when wishes can float along
under a cathedral ceiling of eternal blue.

Yellow lions
jagged leaves like teeth in grass

bitter healing
in their wine blood.

I want there to be more moments
where I can just be

with you all fingers and breath
seeds and air.

Bright white energy
giving way in a puff of shattered stars.

We're always more than just one thing,
pieces of us reaching out to settle

the perfectly green lawns
of paradise.

Sending our inside out,
past what we know

to anywhere we wish.

Dowsing

All I wanna do is go jump in a lake
he tells me

and I can feel it in my hands like the first time
I felt a heartbeat through the cloth

of a t-shirt
too small for me that I still insist on keeping

in my closet like some kind of psycho
who needs to feel like

this is the real world
and things will never change as long as

I don't think about the past
and how much easier it was

when all I had to do was hold my breath
and count to ten

while watching the bubbles
escape through my opening lips

like stars in a country night's blackness
the only light that ever traveled

so far forward so fast
to reach us.

The Great American Eclipse

The August 2017 solar eclipse
had a path of totality that touched 14 states.

A woman in Staten Island
stared too long at the star

probably tempted by the sparkle
of the moon as it cried out in that diamond ring moment.

But she never felt the sting
that left the crescent bite of its nails

deep in the earthy, shadowed
cellular level of her eyes.

In fact, she thought no more of it

until the fog rolled in at the edges
and she began to lose her sight.

Perhaps some sun warmed afternoons
she sits in the darkness and thinks back to the moment

when that same moon shape could be seen
rising on the sidewalk through the leaves

and she wishes she could tell herself
that reflection is magic enough.

We Were Like the Birds

It was always winter
with you and I.

Our bodies shivering, our fingers frozen
but I remember being on fire

when we were like the birds
who follow in the warmth of a train's smoke stack

chasing after each ragged breath
connecting in a gray bridge of exhalation.

I fit just below your chin
a frisson of happiness in your arms.

We were like the birds
whose hearts beat one thousand times a minute

feathers red against the snow,
soul light like molten gold

an early morning star too bright
to stare too long.

Do you still feel it inside
even after all this time?

Prophet

Thought I knew who I was
after all that time trying to find myself.

But I'm still struggling to believe in my daydreams,
those words that once seemed so deep

and now feel like shallow reflections
of something someone, somewhere has already said.

I used to think words could grow wings
if only they were folded just right.

A diary of origami birds
taking to the sky.

Can anyone really describe what love tastes like
when you speak it aloud?

Can I wait a wing beat
before I say it back?

Or will it dry out like red pressed petals
at the back of my throat?

Some people can float in the silence
brought on by a frown.

But I can't handle all that perfect emptiness,
something swells up inside

and I want to follow the birds back to the story's start
and try again.

Acknowledgments

With gratitude to the editors of the following publications where these poems, sometimes in a different form, first appeared:

The Artistic Muse: "Remember Breakfast"

Fox Adoption Magazine: "Nothing/Making" and "We Were Like the Birds"

Miracle Magazine: "On Rice"

The Pacific Northwest Inlander: "The Rabbit" and "Fortuna Major"

the Same: "The Lovers"

Spokane Coeur d'Alene Living Magazine: "Love Awaiting Burial"

West Central Publishing Union (A Division of Spark Central, Spokane): "The Magician"

Early Praise

Ordinary Omens combines earthly beauty with cosmic magic. Each poem contains its own universe, paying tribute to our senses with detailed imagery, and at the same time, reaching out to the mysteries of the universe. The poetry touches the true and authentic inner longings of the readers and carries us toward deeper realms involving the intersection of our own personal language with a new voice from the Muse, the voice of LeAnn Bjerken. The reader will soar on the wings of pure poetry, poetry our world needs now more than ever.

—**Nila J. Webster, author of** *Remember Rain* **and** *Songs of Wonder for the Night Sea Journey*

LeAnn Bjerken's *Ordinary Omens* reads like a book of rituals, potions, incantations, and talismans for conjuring the magic that only domesticity can make. With trusting intimacy and captivating sensuality, Bjerken traces the ecstatic, headlong cycles of desire and fulfillment from which enduring love is spun. Her poems remind us that, in our loving and loved bodies, we are of the same dirt as the earthworm and burrowing rabbit, the same air as the birds, the same water as the minnow *born ready to swim* and make a home in—and of—this world.

—**Jonathan Johnson, author of** *May Is an Island*

LeAnn Bjerken's *Ordinary Omens* opens with a spell and then casts one. The speaker takes us from her birth through key moments in her life, focusing primarily on the experience of falling in love, and these ordinary experiences are made extraordinary through Bjerken's surreal images. One of my favorite poems in this book, "Keep on Floating," feels like a Marc Chagall painting in that it's a real world made less and more real by being tilted sideways:

I stay home to climb the walls with you. / We walk the ceiling / tripping in the door frames / stepping around lights. Reading this book feels like we're in a world that is both familiar and new, made so by the magic of language and love.

—Laura Read, author of *But She Is Also Jane*

About the Author

Originally from Minnesota, **LeAnn Bjerken** holds an MFA in creative writing from Eastern Washington University. A former journalist, freelance writer and mermaid performer, she has temporarily traded her fins for legs in order to better keep up with her daughter. Her poetry has appeared in *Miracle Magazine, The Pacific Northwest Inlander, Spokane Coeur d'Alene Living Magazine,* and online publications including *Devilfish Review, The Artistic Muse, The Lake, Fox Adoption Magazine,* and *Plants & Poetry Journal.* When not out seeking inspiration, she can be found at home snuggling with her husband Steve, daughter Eowyn, and cat Tikki.

About The Poetry Box®

The Poetry Box, a boutique publishing company in Portland, Oregon, provides a platform for both established and emerging poets to share their words with the world through beautiful printed books and chapbooks.

Feel free to visit the online bookstore (thePoetryBox.com), where you'll find more titles including:

A Starved Heart by Genevieve Lardizabol

Break-Up Hair & Other Poems by Grace Richards

What She Was Wearing by Shawn Aveningo Sanders

When All Else Fails by Lana Hechtman Ayers

metal used for beauty alone by Claudia Saleeby Savage

How to Say by Stephanie A. Marcellus

A Nest in the Heart by Vivienne Popperl

This Is the Lightness by Rachel Barton

Self Dissection by Amelia Diaz Ettinger

Fencelines by Angela Hansen

Kansas Reimagined by Anara Guard

The Weight of Clouds by Cathy Cain

Excoriation by Rebecca Smolen

Inside Out by Kirsten Morgan

Dear John— by Laura LeHew

and more . . .

www.ingramcontent.com/pod-product-compliance
Lightning Source LLC
La Vergne TN
LVHW050027080526
838202LV00069B/6957